The Light, the Dark, and the Fog

20 Days of Poems

Karyn Little

BookLeaf Publishing

India | USA | UK

The Light, the Dark, and the Fog

20 Days of Poems

© 2021 Karyn Little

All rights reserved.

No part of this publication may be reproduced, stored
in a retrieval system, or transmitted, in any form or by
any means, electronic, mechanical, photocopying,
recording or otherwise, without the prior written
permission of the presenters.

Karyn Little asserts the moral right to be identified
as author of this work.

Presentation by *BookLeaf Publishing*

Web: www.bookleafpub.com

E-mail: info@bookleafpub.com

ISBN : 9789358362886

First edition 2021

For Mom,

Thanks for always supporting me

Acknowledgements

Starting with the thank-yous…

Alvira Publishing and BookLeaf Publishing, for providing me and many other writers around the world with this amazing opportunity. It came at just the right time in my life.

My psychologist and my psychiatrist. Thank you for encouraging me to get back to writing, and for your guidance as I've continued to navigate life with a brain like mine.

My dear friend, Shannon, for gushing over my work every time I started experiencing imposter syndrome. You're great at making me feel more talented than I really am.

My wonderful coworkers at Techboomers, for always supporting my writing goals. Thanks for showing me that positive workplaces exist.

Lastly, my amazing family. Thank you for always supporting me and everything I do. I hope I've made you proud. Also, sorry I didn't tell you about this until it was already a thing.

Preface

This was never an item on the bucket list. My poetry is something that I've always kept to myself, often in a notebook in my bedside table that I reserved for moments when I needed a creative release. I never thought I would be comfortable sharing it with the world.

The poems in this collection are totally raw, written over the course of 20 days. I wanted to use this challenge to show what I feel are the phases I typically experience as someone with mental illness: light, dark, and fog. What I've written might not be perfect, but I hope within them you're able to find comfort or some degree of understanding.

If there's anything I want you to take away from my poems, it's that life is one big cycle. When you find yourself caught in the dark, wait for the fog, then venture forward into the light. It will be there for you when you're ready.

1. Light

Warm air

and sunny skies.

The cliché exists today

in and out of my mind.

There's an unexpected pleasantness

found in this weighted blanket of humidity

and familiarity;

peace,

calm,

happiness,

comfort,

progress,

success,

hope.

All in a single visit

to this beach town I once called

home.

The switch has been turned on.

2. Date Night

In this moment

everything feels right.

Our smiles compete

to be the biggest

as the butterflies dance

in our stomachs.

It's still the early days

of this journey together.

Yet, we already feel so

complete.

These moments we've dreamed about

for years on end are finally here.

Let me stay close to you

beyond this date night

that my unconscious mind

has created for us

again.

I don't want to wake up.

I'm not ready for this night to end.

3. Completion

And just like that

the world sits still.

There are no anxieties on

today's to-do list,

or yearning for

the moments that will come

after the anxieties have been

checked off.

There's just calm.

A never-ending tranquility

that goes on

and on

beyond the foreseeable.

I am relaxed,

and I finally feel safe.

Why do I want something more?

4. Warmth

You asked me if I was cold.

I told you

no

even though you insisted

there was a chill in the air.

Surrounded by faces and

kitten snuggles and

TV specials and

the embodiment of a

lazy Sunday;

this is the warmest I've felt in months.

5. Happier

The music plays on repeat

three different songs,

all with the same name.

I'm trying to live in the present,

allowing each beat to carry me forward,

but it's the lyrical content that keeps

catapulting me back

into the past.

Is this what I was supposed to wish for

him?

I have a question I need to ask.

Dear Ed,

Dear Dan,

Dear Olivia,

It's been ten years since I let him go.

Why don't I feel happier now?

6. Sarnia

There is light everywhere.

In this moment, I am

grateful.

I'm far away from the things that

hurt me

and the things that

worry me.

I'm awake

and I'm smiling,

comfortable in my surroundings.

This is where I come to escape.

This is where I come to heal.

I'm holding on to this

with the tightest grip.

I never want to let go.

7. Dark

What is there to be seen?

Beyond the blankets cocooning me

and the blinds shut tight

as my eyes,

I'm convinced there is nothing.

Nothing purposeful.

Nothing joyful.

Nothing meaningful.

Just a repetitive cycle

of this bland survival game

I keep playing.

Even if I went looking

there wouldn't be any others

on the shelf.

The switch has been turned off.

8. Ticking Clock

Time goes by

and I'm still

here.

Tick-

Tock.

Tick-

Tock.

I want to do more,

but everything moves

too fast.

Tick-

Tock.

Tick-

Tock.

Please slow down.

I'm trying to

keep up.

Tick-

Tock.

Tick-

Tock.

I thought I'd be

further along by

now.

Tick-tock.

Tick-tock.

I feel like I'm losing

the best years of my

life.

Tick-tock tick-tock tick-tock

Tick-tock tick-tock tick-tock

How do I make time stop?

9. Forgiveness Therapy

I'm still hurting.

I want to let go

without needing to forgive you.

I want to spew hate

without the weight of my anger.

I want to point fingers at your flaws

without pointing three at myself.

I want your legacy to crumble

without falling down with you.

I want to walk by your door

without the memories flooding back.

I want to take everything I've learned from
you

without showing you any bit of gratitude.

Why am I the only one

that has to better myself?

10. 1:11

I've been told it means

my desires are manifesting.

But I've seen this synchronicity

flashing optimistically at me

almost every day

for months.

He still isn't here.

11. Anger

The only color I see

in the replays of your

faded memory

is red.

12. Waste

Wasted days

turn into

wasted nights.

The clock doesn't care

how you spent your

1440 minutes.

There's no checklist of fulfillment

ensuring you filled your minutes

with joy,

or progress,

or something reminiscent

of the meaning of life

before it moves on

to the next.

Time waits for no one.

No exceptions.

It will happily carry on,

watching as you

waste away.

13. Anxiety

I've lost so much

because I was

afraid.

The fear worked

like super glue

securing my feet

firmly

to the ground

and keeping my mouth shut

tight

—lips forming a guarding smile—

as if to say,

"I'm keeping you safe."

No reaching for opportunities.

No standing up for myself.

No going after him.

My one that got away.

It made me choose the pain

from the emptiness

over the pain

from the rejection.

14. Fog

I want to see the morning.

I want to know what's hidden

behind the cool sheet of clouds.

I think whatever it is

is warm,

and beautiful,

and something I'm meant to find.

I just need to wake myself up.

I need my eyes to know

they can open

and stay open.

I need to rid my head of

the groggy weight

that keeps it pinned to the pillow.

I need my body to know it's able to

sit up,

and stand up,

and leave this room,

and dance among the cracks of light

that escape through the morning clouds,

welcoming the day.

I need my mind to know,

despite whatever is waiting for me

when the stratus clears,

it's going to be okay.

I just wish I knew how.

Something's wrong with the circuitry.

15. Document

Last edit was 2 hours ago.

Last shower was 2 days ago.

Last good night's sleep was 2 weeks ago.

Last sense of control was 2 months ago.

Last time I felt hope was 2 years ago.

Track Changes.

16. T****

You used the word

"excalibur"

and I knew my words

could never come close

to the way you create

fantasies

in lyrical tongue.

I know I should stop trying

to write romantic tragedies

about you

and what I remember of

the way your eyes

made me feel.

I should rip out the page,

crumple it up,

and throw it away;

starting again with a

blank page.

But I still have lots of

ink left

for you.

And even though

there's no reason to believe

I'm anything more than a

tertiary character

in the story of your summer,

part of me wonders

if sometimes

you pick up the pen

and write

fantasies

from your memory

of me.

17. Labeled

Knowing isn't

half the battle.

I still wake up most days

feeling stuck in

a body that rejects

the very idea of

proper care

and accomplishment.

At least I know it's

not my fault.

18. Healing

There are moments

where I'm just

OK

and that itself is

something

to be proud of.

I've had to

convince myself

that I'm allowed

a period of

rest

after time spent

running in the rain.

19. Our Truth

When the world

tries to tell you

your life

should be

different.

Repeat:

I'm still ill

but I still live.

20. Life's Work

My brain is a

highly-skilled artist,

capable of drawing

obstacles

convincingly detailed

with shading

and stippling.

The doctor gave me

an eraser

and told me to

change what

I saw.

"It's just pencil,

not ink."

I often find new

optical illusions

she drew in

the margins.

I try to erase them

from the pages of

my story,

but too much

pressure was used

and faint outlines

remain.

I didn't ask to co-author

this story with her,

but maybe her work

is supposed to be there.

Maybe she adds

something

that better explains

why things happened

the way they did.

I still try to

erase her artwork,

but I won't rip

the pages

trying to make it

go away.

I've accepted that

it's just the way

she is.

It doesn't matter

if she insists on

doodling

throughout this journey.

She'll never be able to

fill the pages.

Only I can do that

with words.

www.ingramcontent.com/pod-product-compliance
Lightning Source LLC
LaVergne TN
LVHW021254200726
843509LV00012B/1670